Gloria
for seven voices

Words from the Ordinary of the Mass

CLAUDIO MONTEVERDI
Edited by John Rutter

Glory to God in the highest,

OXFORD UNIVERSITY PRESS, MUSIC DEPARTMENT, GREAT CLARENDON STREET, OXFORD OX2 6DP

* The Cs in S.1 and Vln.1 have a ♯ added by hand in the source, which avoids the false relation with the bass, but is not necessarily preferable. The source copy (in the library of the University of Wrocław) has a number of accidentals added in ink by an unknown, probably 17th-century hand; some are valid, others dubious.

*These four bars are in the alto part-book (probably a printer's error), but it is suggested they be reassigned to basses 1 and 2 as shown.

* The ♯ added by hand in the source. ♮ may be considered preferable.

H 122 Tutti

S. Gra - ti - as a - gi - mus ti - bi pro-pter ma - gnam,

A. Gra - ti - as a - gi - mus ti - bi pro-pter ma - gnam,

T. Gra - ti - as a - gi - mus ti - bi pro-pter ma - gnam,

T. Gra - ti - as a - gi - mus ti - bi pro-pter ma - gnam glo - -

B. Gra - ti - as a - gi - mus ti - bi pro-pter ma - gnam,

B. Gra - ti - as a - gi - mus ti - bi pro-pter ma - gnam,

We give thanks . . .   *to you*   *because of your great glory.*

130

S. pro-pter ma - gnam,   pro-pter

A. pro-pter ma - gnam,   pro-pter

T. pro-pter ma - gnam,   pro-pter

T. - - - ri-am tu - am,   pro-pter

B. pro-pter ma - gnam,   pro-pter

B. pro-pter ma - gnam glo - - - - - ri-am tu - -

[5] ♯

O Lord God,

* The small notes here and in bars 154, 166, and 192 are editorial ornaments. They may be sung, if preferred, instead of the plain notes.

Lamb of God, Son of the Father,

You who take away . . .

the sins of the world,   *have mercy,*

have mercy upon us.

* This G is probably correct, though it could be a misprint for A one note higher.

† Voice parts have 𝄐 in source.

* Voice parts have 𝄐 in source.

* Original note value ○ in all voices except for T1, which is unaltered.

24

ISBN 0-19-341785-5

Printed and bound in Great Britain by
Caligraving Limited Thetford Norfolk

9 780193 417854